Yellow Trophies

Other Books by Thomas Kielty Blomain

Gray Area, Nightshade Press, 2004

Blues From Paradise, Foothills Publishing, 2014

Yellow Trophies

Thomas Kielty Blomain

NYQ Books™

The New York Quarterly Foundation, Inc.
New York, New York

NYQ Books™ is an imprint of The New York Quarterly Foundation, Inc.

The New York Quarterly Foundation, Inc.
P. O. Box 2015
Old Chelsea Station
New York, NY 10113

www.nyq.org

First Edition

Set in New Baskerville

Layout by Raymond P. Hammond

Cover Design by Raymond P. Hammond

Cover and Author Photographs by Mark Migliore

Library of Congress Control Number: 2016939029

ISBN: 978-1-63045-029-8

Special thanks to Raymond Hammond
and conversations they should give trophies for.

Yellow Trophies

Contents

Theories

Myths

Heirlooms

Apologies

Scatter these well-meant idioms
Into the smoky spring that fills
The suburbs, where they will be lost.
There are no trophies of the sun.

Hart Crane, from "Praise for an Urn"

For Michael
  And Jessica
    And my sisters
      And my ancestors
        And my hometown

Theories

Trickle Down Theory

Don't look up
Beholden to their theory

The simple truth to it really
Is this

What trickles down
Will be golden
Only if it's piss

Saint Obvious

All the business of popes
And rules of religion

Who follows what book better
Who reads the best

Between lines written by
Who knows who or when

And which collector of souls
Can hold his trophy higher

It's really a simple thing
God damn it

Just look around
No one should get it wrong

What to Worry About

Things not to worry about include
Being killed by a terrorist or
Attacked by a shark

The odds are in your favor
That neither will happen to you

Things to worry however include
Being terrorized by relentless news
Of all the wrong things

And the greedy machinations of those
You will never even meet

Machiavelli's Haircut

Machiavelli got a new haircut
And wears a different kind of suit,
Not to say a disguise,
But he looks like a regular, modern guy
At the meetings of the Medici types

He knew they'd pay for his lunch, too,
For sharing his gift of cunning advice
On how to keep winning in spite
Of the disgruntlement in the streets

Popular through the centuries,
He's an invited guest again and again
To the conference rooms of all sides,
As he has been throughout history

But ultimately,
The Americans became his favorites,
With their unlimited supply of fat envelopes
And shadowy networks, connecting
Even political enemies, in a perfect confluence
Of deceitful possibilities

His tricks, revised and refined,
Through years of misfeasance and outright lies,
Work every time they call on him

And the people line up behind
Any anointed figurehead, just as directed,
Once all competitors and genuine threats
Are destroyed by the complicit press

The populace, calmed by notions of choice,
Vote against their interests every time,
Baited by easy scapegoats and ghosts of tradition

Then they go home peacefully,
Incredibly, quietly convinced
That their Constitution always miraculously wins,
And that the hero who finally comes in first
Has been duly chosen by them
And is truly one of their own

Reality Theater

We don't really need
Or even necessarily expect
To prevail in any actual conflict

We're Americans after all
Always victorious later on in our films

With no second thoughts given
To losses for how fast cowboys can draw

Before any scene even concludes
The line between Hollywood
And Columbine further blurs
With each third page death

And yet our tears seem real
As only the best actors can do

Glamorizing yellow police tape
Like red carpet velvet ropes

We stand in our bloodline
At the Cineplex
Armed to the teeth with treats
To see clear-cut villains
Get their due and to cheer
For the holograms of the giant heroes
Who kill them and put the evil-doers
Out of our misery

But sometimes we're forced to wait impatiently
At the shiny turnstiles just like regular folks
For some harried usher to show us to our seats

Playing Chess with a Terrorist

I was talking to a guy who served in Iraq
As a guard in the palace of the fallen regime,
Overthrown by the American military

While his colleagues searched the countryside
For phantom weapons of mass destruction,
He played chess with someone we called a terrorist

Not so much an enemy now as just a routine captive,
A prisoner, bored inside walls he himself once oversaw
As a figure of great power and wealth, like a knight

Barriers of culture tamed by this ancient game,
They moved their pieces, reading each other's faces
And whatever other clues their gestures might betray

This "high value detainee" always won, he said;
No one ever beat him, even though—to his captors' surprise—
He always seemed to play by the age-old rules

That man is dead, of course; and that place, checked in blood,
Is like a scattered board today, rampant without kings—
All stray bishops, rooks, and pawns chasing something to win

On the Recent Suicide Bombings

In the middle of the day
The night came

Dressed like any other guy except
With a loaded vest under his coat

So no one would know in advance
His plan to channel the darkness

Through the passages of a book
As mistaken as all the rest

In a busy city street
Finally peaceful in the wake of the past

Amid the rubble and smoke of the aftermath
His bones hold no glory among the fallen stones

Which will simply be rebuilt into something else
His brothers may hate just as well

And again sometime another may try
To annihilate what is left of our grand effort

Exploding the remnants of the soul of man after
Centuries of commands from the bad gods we've made

Whose languages can't be translated anyway
Through any of the relics or paper scrolls we wave around

And no amount of killing can make us one
And no rebuilding can ever make us whole

Until we can look toward the indifferent heavens and see
No mortal truth can shine like the heedless sun

Dogmatism

The answer is given
Even before any question
Is asked

Somewhere in the past
Someone who knew better than you
Already decided on the choreography

So like dancers whose feet
Are pinned to the floor
We sway on a cramped stage

In the room we were herded
Believing we are truly moving
To the music of the universe

Singing along all the same words
From a page of hymns we were handed
By someone who came along first

Bumper Stickers

There's so much to infer
From bumper stickers
On the backs of cars

Stuck in traffic
With someone's politics or religion
Summarized in front of you

Mostly you'll find you disagree
Maybe seek to construct deeper stories
Of these drivers and passengers

Sometimes they're funny
Sometimes they make you mad
Sometimes you may even fantasize

About stepping on the gas
And crashing into them
For the chance to find out for sure

Who they are
And why they believe what they do
Enough to label themselves that way

And through some randomness
Of Chaos Theory force you
To see their petulant beliefs

When all you wanted to do
Was to get where you're going
And arrive with your own sticky thoughts

Bullhorns

When the crackpots talk about "leadership"
What they mean is a call to war
First thing
No other issues to explore

Sure
There are times in life you'll be forced
To do things you hate to have to do
One of which of course is to participate in killing
Which really should be the last resort

But when an occasion arises
An incident or instance
For the bullhorns to fire up
And the steel wheels of expensive machines
Which do not like to idle
Start grinding into action
These people will find the right slogans
To manufacture
And sing like varsity fight songs at a game

Only after their own sons and daughters
Are safely sequestered away from any threats
And the actual business of bullets and bayonets
Is left to someone else
Whom they will then disingenuously refer to
As heroes

While the sad truth of it is
That only the death of everyone else
Could ever make the singular world safe
For freedom and democracy and the free trade
They claim to generate by proclamation
Directly from heaven

But all the sides have their gods
And the odds are they will never get along
With their different accents and scripts read aloud
Never tenuously
From various pulpits and soap boxes
With their words being shouted
Through similar bullhorns
Probably all made by the same company

Wall with One Side

You can build a wall of words
So high you can't reach up
To lay another row

And you may look at this wall
And decide it's high enough
No one can get over

And you might admire your wall
At least for a little while
Until you ultimately realize

There you are alone
And you don't remember
The other side

Oral History

I've been reading lately
How they've dug up
The bones and gold,
Coins and combs,
Even long boats
From old tombs
In Northern Europe and
Along the Baltic coast,
Holding treasures from
As far away as Constantinople;
How the crusty remains
From these elaborate graves
Explain a curious culture
That wrote nothing down
Of their forays and raids
Into distant places,
Encountering odd religions
Of kings and caliphates and popes,
All of whom used written words
So history would find in their favor.
Later, once they were Christianized
And forced to stop eating horses,
Their burials became routine,
Just another chore you have to do
With the dead, nothing anyone
Would want to read about anyway
Now that they had begun
To write things down

Evolution

Consider Adam and Eve
Chased through Eden
In those fundamentalist renditions
Where it all started at once
Six thousand years ago

Escaping Tyrannosaurus Rex
Only to be tricked into ruin
By a single snake
With a great pitch
And a simple treat

And even God
Who supposedly knew everything
Had to ask
Why aren't you running around naked
Like I planned?

The husband was ashamed to admit
His weakness
Blaming that inadvertent wife of his
That bitch
With her persuasive wiles
Obviously unsatisfied with his gift of ribs
Who fell for the glib serpent's shtick
And the history of scapegoats began

And man
Though clothed in knowledge now
Still stands stupefied
At random apple pulpit huckster carts
To deny things we learned the hard way
About dinosaurs and talking snakes and paradise

The metaphor by the clever author of Genesis
Lost in the vaporized garden
Long since synthesized
Into a giant corporate orchard of forbidden trees
Deep under the soil of whose roots
The bones of Paradoxus still fertilize
The savory fruits of our favorite myths

Divine Invention

I often wonder if one guy came up with it,
Or if it was like a committee, or maybe
A number of individuals independently
Arrived at the idea, and then later shared
Their common notion when they finally met

Of course, we'll never know for sure;
It was too long ago
And no one kept good records back then

But I bet it started first when someone
Needed something new to blame,
And then elevated it with a twist of praise

It's possible he was out, getting home late
Without the carcass he sought,
Without the meat and fur she expected,
And he had to explain to his angry, hungry woman
How a magical distraction suddenly appeared,
As he knew from experience, just by her look,
That she'd accept none of his routine excuses again

Or it might have been the woman, who had spent
Some unaccounted for time away from the cave,
And when she returned, she had to find a way
To still her crazy man's raving with a fabulous tale

Quickly, right off the top of her head, she invented
A nameless, heroic stranger who had saved her
From some grave danger when she got lost while
Trying to find something nice to bring back for him

She clutched a sharp rock and scratched a vague image
On the wall as proof, making her patent "How Dare You
Question Me" face. With her hands on her hips, her hair
All wild like a survivor, she knew how to teach him a lesson

Then, with a private smile, as he stood there in awe
Of her story, she went on about concocting some kind of gruel
To get her angry, hungry fool to shut up about it now
And just believe in this glorious, powerful beast
That lived somewhere out there and seemed to own it all

She always knew she could get him to fall for anything
If she gave him something to eat

How Long It Takes to Say One Thing Right

The place between
What you did in the bathroom of your youth
And the book you wish to fill with something good

The countless folded napkins
You scribbled your wild genius on
Use them to wipe up your vomit now

The whiskey-toned images
That came to you like heroic ghosts
An hour after the bars closed

And those that visited you
After every verbose boner told you
You were in love

It all needs to ferment
In a box somewhere
While decades have their way

And if you ever see those poems again
Have tissues and a pack of matches nearby
So you can cry while you burn them

And try not to count out the time
Or the number of flames it takes
Just to say one thing right

Insurance Seminar

The subject is planning
Contingencies and exigencies
Scribbled on a big white board up front
A blacklist of potential catastrophes

The frenetic speaker calmly answers
Earnest questions that meekly follow
About how we can be so sure
Fielding them with a nod and folded brow

We have tables and charts and graphs and facts
Gleaned from the hidden underwriting gods
Incontrovertible evidence of life expectancy
Clean data and formulas of the odds

How many of a thousand will live how long
And how many houses will burn down
The only insoluble to account
Is the particulars of which ones and when

Among other incalculable questions
An autumn day like this squandered
In rows with hotel tablets and plastic pens
Listening to grim statistics so evenly pondered

No one will ever even try to equate it
Indeed most would never admit to misspent time
In this vortex of urgency and coffee cups
And the quiet yet hurried bagel line

Finally once outside the conference center
After such a day of numbers and catch phrases
Mortality becomes clearer as the sun goes down
And the stack of glossy handout pages

Carefully placed on the back seat of the car
Find their way to the floor in disarray
As you slam on the brakes to avoid hitting
Some dark thing that ran across the road

A Comedian Commits Suicide

Funny
When you're not alone

Their laughter is like fuel
That burns hottest when their backs are turned

When doors close behind them
And your lips suddenly don't know what to do

And the ache you've been joking about pounds
Where no medicine could ever reach

And you sit there momentarily
In the vortex of intolerable silence you've always known

Before breaching everything they ever thought of you
With a punchline you've been waiting to deliver

Since even before the first time
You were forced to make them laugh

Music of Our Common Disaster

Distant sirens in the rain
Play a melody of catastrophe

A melancholy arpeggio in the scale
Of the symphony of the moment

It is someone's disaster soloing
Out from somewhere in the choir

Sung among the theme
Of our common song

How long we may wonder
Before the coda comes to us

And our turn in the chorus
We all have our time to sing

Feng Shui

We save all the wrong things,
Clutter shelves with stuff
We believe we need to keep

The dust ring where something once was
Tells a better story than whatever
Was there before it went missing

You fill in the blank from your soul,
Leaving no image blurred in mind
After the subtraction and even find

Everything is better for its loss.
They call it Feng Shui in those
Books that smell like incense

But I think I just like the holes,
Maybe even the dust,
And the rest of the story untold

Trophy for Participating

You made it through youth
Even with whatever scars
The orphaning
Then parenthood
At least so far
To reach this "middle age"
As it's called

Your extra weight
Your glasses
Dental work
The relentless bills you pay
And taxes
A closet with some silk in it
Boxes of poems on the floor

Your moot recollections
Revised as necessary to suit your day
Every single thing more debatable
Including all the songs you ever sung
And every drawing you threw away

Add it up in just another solitary hour
And see what kind of award
You can make yourself believe in

Knowing as you finally do now
There is no trophy for any of this
And no such thing as winning for long

An Empty Shelf

An empty shelf is a curiosity,
Particularly when dust is left there
To outline the space
Where something once was

Picture frames perhaps and
Books or mementoes from trips,
Awards of some past glory

It's especially odd in your own house
Rather than a stranger's.
That story is even better

Wiped clean, it loses its magic,
Removing the residue
For imagination to fill in the blanks
That might as well have been true

You can probe its meaning repeatedly,
Using your whole history like a tongue
Seeking a missing tooth

If anyone ever asks
Don't be too quick to explain.
What business is it of theirs anyway?

Unable for whatever reason
To ever put anything else on it,
Just leave it alone to inertly define
All the vital things you might have done

Myths

Crossing the Myth Field

Somewhere beyond actual memory,
In a past we may not have really had,
We stood and looked out across a field
Of grass and goldenrod

Maybe we were children then,
Or maybe we were already old;
Either way we gazed across this mythic field
Of tall grass and goldenrod

It beckoned us the way a challenge does
To whatever was on the other side;
It was not even ours to guess just then
What might be the sweet place in our lives

We arrived covered with actual spiders
Who were webbed all through the grass,
But we laughed and picked them off each other,
Wiser as we looked back

Because somehow as we ran we found
The stories others before us told
Were often false and even mocked the worth
Of crossing through weeds and goldenrod

And the exaggerated threat of the spiders
Became an inside joke to those who came across,
And we could scoff and shout like no others
Because we had learned the truth

The Blue Mist

The Blue Mist was the specter of the murdered witch,
Burned alive in her cottage by villagers, no one could say when.
That was the legend anyway

More clinically surmised, it was just the mixture
Of green growth and moisture in those hot summer nights,
Creating an aura over the remains of some old stone house

A spruce-colored glow every one of us claimed to see
At the site of our wild parties, when the music from our cars
Would wake her in horror like the mob came back again

Far down a rocky road, lacking light even in the day,
It was a beautifully secluded place
To elude parents and police

Peaceful, except for the stories
And occasional screams from out of the trees,
But no one would confess any kind of fear of ghosts

Yet all sound would abruptly cease
And we would listen breathlessly
When someone said, "What's that noise?"

We never found out,
And today the space has been bulldozed,
Planted with little mansions that will never explain

How that mythical witch stays with us,
However far from her graveyard
We ever get the chance to go

A Beautiful and Unsafe Place

We broke the law
Swimming in the reservoir
Ignoring the No Trespassing signs
Out of sight of the road

The legend of something big
Living in the green water
Frightened no one
Not believing in such creatures
Feeding on young divers
At least not in this small town

Hearts carved in old trees still there
Reaching over the dirt trail
A rocky path to nowhere
That was everywhere back then

Pulled to this shoreline again
So many years later
I think of the friends who gathered here
All who have disappeared

Victims of monsters
We never could have conjured
As we ran from those police cars
That came to scatter us away
From this beautiful and unsafe place

On an Old Photo of the Crew

This old photo of bad boys
Years ago outside the school
Now most of them dead
Or gone good

Shoulder to shoulder
In black-and-white weather
Making one last stand together
Before the counting began

Mischief in the faces
A humorous arrogance in the stance
The photographer later hanged himself
Before he even had a chance to fail

Inside that building there were dirty looks
Uncertain glances from most of the girls
Our names all famous as they hung in the air
From the loudspeakers in the halls

With pockets full of contraband
Between false fire alarms
Slumped in the back of classrooms
Waiting for a diversion

To bolt out to the cars in the lot
Lighting cigarettes on the way
Whether being chased or not
We moved with grace and speed

Racing off to something else we shouldn't do
Not noting anything in the rearview mirror then
To even hint at what we would spend
Forever losing from that point on

Shooting Mary

Three teenage boys out in dad's car at night,
Cruising with 22s and a rural rage they shared,
To shoot Mary or any black-faced lamp jockey
They might find anywhere outside, coast down
The long hill road, past the 1950s homes,
Peaceful and quiet, with vigilant yards
And yellow bug lamps, out of place now in fall

Somewhere near the flower bed, the short grotto
Arches over her shape. Inside a stout blue shell,
A pasty Mary clasps her hands, as if awaiting the light

It comes from the car as the driver slows down,
Elbowing back his anxious friends, knocking off
His remaining beer. "Watch that, you asshole,"
He scolds, shoving a stray barrel away from his ear

Two of them hustle out onto the deserted road,
All eyes on Mary as the driver holds a flashlight beam.
She prays, sickly white in her contrived little shrine
As the boys with the guns line her up in their sights

The loud pops are swallowed by the thick autumn night
As Mary's plaster head blows obligingly apart.
"Jesus Christ! See that one? Blew the head right off!"
To whoops and hollers, their stifled rebel yells,
The merry marauders get away, popping a trinity
Of fresh, cold beers, happy to not get caught

Not that they ever gave it a great deal of thought,
The whole notion of virgin birth and whatnot.
These missions were completely without religion,
Although they never believed much in Mary either way

Boys Will Be Boys

My G.I. Joes would kick in the door
Of my sister's Barbie house
When it was least expected
In a stunning blitzkrieg raid

Ken, weak and inept, was slain instantly
Where he sat watching the little plastic TV

Naturally, Barbie was taken away
For the men's pleasure later,
After they looted her tiara
And stole her rubber car

They'd tear around the playroom floor,
Between the train set and the Easy-Bake Oven,
Running over any other toys that got in the way

Until Donna burst in screaming at me,
Squealing how I was just the worst
And about all the bad I always did

Then, of course, our parents would come in
With stern looks and scolding words to break it up,
Mostly because they didn't like the noise

I'd just innocently shrug,
Pointing to those guilty soldiers,
Who seemed to have a cold will of their own

And I could honestly say, "It wasn't me,"
Knowing they'd believe it, because after all,
Boys will be boys

Smoke and Clouds

I know how bad it is
They said it since I was a kid
In a kitchen full of cigarettes
And in the car and in the den
In the bedrooms and especially
In the barroom downstairs

Now in a different house
In the same polluted town
Years later in this fated middle age
Still surrounded by smoke
I deliberately mistake for clouds
Because I love their Rorschach shapes
Even those billowing from the distant reactor
Along the river to the south

Back when they made me kneel
To pray or confess or repent
They used to say that's where heaven is
Behind glorious gates you can't see
From our place down here
Yet I always thought I could see them

These days of course I don't believe
In either heaven or confession
But I still believe in clouds
Even with all the dirty ways we create them
With our science and our business and our mouths

And maybe even more so now
In whatever sort of atonement can possibly be found
In their moody and graceful and unrepentant forms

Yggdrasil

Tall enough even back then for a god to hang from
Seeming to defy the implacable seasons that drum
Whole forests into submission to shed their cloaks
Stronger I supposed than other maples or locusts or oaks

This one held up the sky in my childhood's yard
A millennium ago when any voyage was hard
Like the four long blocks to my parochial school and back
Where they told us how only one god made light from black

And created the trees and everything else all at once
All the fish in the seas and all the animals man hunts
Out of a vast swirl of nothing that finally ended here
At this tree in front of my house which to me did appear

To reach much higher than any dreams I might ever have had
Overarching the neighborhood legends of good and bad
I never saw the top of it until I came back almost old
Just to look at it again and try once more to behold

The notion of such a sentry posted at my boyhood's door
Guarding all the things I knew enough to care for
As I was yet to learn of my deeper ancestors' heaven
We moved away from there before I turned eleven

So I had to return to that lost place later just to see
How much magic can truly inhabit a common tree
And there it was stretching straight up into the sky
It had not fallen and I realized neither had I

With whatever knowledge I was able to gain
From childhood on about holiness and love and pain
 I could spot the top of this tree even as tall as it rises
And see all the gods hang there now in various disguises

Coincidental Penance

I didn't go looking for it
But coincidentally because of a meeting I had today
I came face to face with my grade school
And the church right across the street

Expecting echoes and ghosts when I looked up
Of those nuns and the times I was put to my knees
There were only these two brick buildings
With new children walking in between them

I tried to conjure the dead for a moment
Because I remember weather like this very well
Filing from desks to pews and back again
In a uniform like the one I've worn ever since

Maybe the walls actually look kind of shabby now
Sort of run down and un-mystical somehow or perhaps
A corrupted memory of it all is to blame
By both the years here and the years away

What I know for sure is they don't slam kids around
Like those black-robed women used to do to us
And the only confessionals you're forced to enter now
Are those no scripted penance can ever free you from

Lesson from First Grade

I went to first grade in a dark suit
With two-toned shoes, carrying
A brief case. There's a picture
Somewhere of me heading out,
Like a little boss to the office,
Five years old and ready to start
Ordering people around

I had no idea then what that meant.
The only nun I had ever met
Was my great aunt when she'd visit
From the convent, to take the sacrament
Of spiked egg nog before playing
Christmas carol songs on the piano
In those big, off-key family sing-alongs

When my dad's high Irish tenor
Would soar over all the other voices
Like a rampant bird, trilling out endings
As the final notes faded, then refilling
Everyone's glass in a hurry, the way
A gracious host should before the next
Rendition everyone loved of Silent Night

So when I was introduced to a new
Shrouded woman, I had no reason to be
Timid. I guess I thought they'd all
Behave like tipsy pianists, the way things
Went on during the holiday pageants
In my house. I didn't learn until later that
My great aunt had been retired from her post

Apparently she had lost her ability
To control the rowdy kids who mostly
Sat quietly at their desks. Never once did she
Hit me with a stick, even when I deliberately
Sang her holy songs all wrong, trying to make
A joke of it, as I always did. But I gleaned fast
That these sisters could read your thoughts

And mine always wandered off the pages
Of the catechisms they taught in tense and
Stuffy rooms. I had no notion then of doom,
Until that ruler came down in an ambush,
Knocking me back from whatever daydream
I was wishing myself to be a victor in, to make me
Pick up quickly wherever the last kid left off

Memoir of a Holy Youth

I was circumcised and baptized
Before I could even say a word

I don't remember but I'm sure
I cried both times

Next thing I knew I was dressed
In a suit and sent to sit in a room
With what I think was a woman
Draped in a gown with a headdress on
Wrapped in a rosary bandoleer
With a crucifix that hung like a key
Wielding a stick like a sword
Tapping on a black chalkboard
Always in One Two Three

We were led back and forth
In perfect symmetry
From this school to its church
In utter silence with folded hands
To sit and stand and kneel in pews
While they swung gas canisters
Of incense and chanted Latin phrases

None of us knew what they meant
Something about someone being dead
To save us from our sins
Which we would learn to invent
Just to be able to confess them
Under duress again and again

And later at home just before dinner
I'd recite by rote a grace poem
For gifts we were about to receive
Then I'd go play with my little army men
Killing the gray ones in waves
As my side drove toward inevitable victory

Until they made me go to bed
Where in my sleep I'd have these dreams
I had no real control over either

Detente

We used to hide from the public school kids
In our maroon blazers and ties, back in 1966.
They weren't "Catholic," whatever that meant,
And they dressed like they were always going out to play

Occasionally we'd encounter them during the school year
In the blocks between their Longfellow and our St. Paul's.
Certain of differences we couldn't detect, aside from attire,
There must have been some sort of defect
Unclarified to us by our nuns, so we kept our distance

They seemed like perfectly okay kids to me,
But there had to be something to the warnings
We received about them, the subtle pressures
Not to mingle

They had the playground behind their school building,
With swings and sliding boards, see-saws and a merry-go-round.
The only things we had other than our uniforms
Were the church across the street and a lone basketball hoop
On a pole in the parking lot, without a ball to jump for.
Even then, I thought it was all completely unfair

And in the summer, they made colorful lanyards there,
Twining vinyl threads into necklaces with little silver clips
On the ends, at a big picnic table, where they all seemed
To have what looked to be very normal fun

And although I never saw a single crucifix
Hanging from any of them, I admit,
I thought they were pretty damn cool,
And I wished I could make one with them

Outnumbered

There we were
With the hammer of Thor
Minding our own business
Raiding and pillaging villages
In places they didn't expect us
When suddenly their god
Who was said to favor peace
Raised great armies to defeat us
And even worse tried to lead us
To their churches once their swords
And shields outnumbered ours
To make us kneel and bow
Blessing us with our own water
In some kind of conquest
Most of us never thought to fight for

A Bone to Pick

Yesterday they brought the shin bone
Of Mary Magdalene to Honesdale, PA.
Hundreds of believers lined the church pews
To view the touring relic's Mass

No matter that it could never be
Confirmed at last as hers,
Questions of faith always burn
Unasked and unanswered

And yet television cameras panned
Over rows of lowered heads, mostly gray
Before the special glass display case
Containing the purported bit of ancient saint

A photograph of two priests kissing an ornate cloth
Made today's front page of The Scranton Times-Tribune,
A garish silver cross dangling in the empty space
Between their heads bowing before the old chip of bone

Climbing the Culm Bank

They used to say how that black mountain
Would swallow us whole
Then close its mouth to leave no trace

All those kids they told us
Disappeared into the guts of the culm pile
Right at the base of Delaware Street

But this silly adult lie failed repeatedly
And we would climb up the long dirty rise
Unfooled in our maroon blazers
And clip-on ties after school

Just to look down from the forbidden height
Upon the clumsy maze that was
The gritty town's rows of angled rooftops
And chimneys smoking over sepia trees

From there the gray city was ours
Full of all dead ends as far as you could see

And no one we knew of was ever eaten
By the vast dump of our town's past waste
Nor for that matter either saved
By our parents' protective lies

Context Clues

Between the mountain
And the city buildings,
The highway
And the University,
Book shelves
And kitchen pots,
Imagination
And actual history,
Leaning guitars
And unfinished art,
The calendar pages
Peeling off,
Gestures of hands,
Eyes and mouths,
People we know, or don't,
And those we forgot about
Or are related to,
Including the deceased
And their unsaid last words,
A definition of home
Haphazardly arranges itself,
The way some poems curiously
Narrate a path to a place
You just feel as you go along,
In a language perhaps
That taunts your fluency,
But which you knew
Even before it was over with,
Was exactly right somehow

Marionette

One day you go into town
And suddenly it's years later.
Your old friends are fat and bald
And have nothing new to say.
The ladies at the bank don't laugh
Anymore until after you've gone,
And you're standing there alone,
Out in the familiar street
Like a marionette
You once held the strings for,
Just waiting now
For a strong enough wind
To push you along the sidewalk
You know every single crack in

How to Believe in Ghosts

Beneath a tree in the park
On a Sunday afternoon,
Under a sky blue in ways
Few of us understand,
The trail of summer foreboding
What doesn't belong,
He etched his own name
With a shotgun barrel
In the pantheon of grief.
Last time I saw him,
He was still laughing
At my disbelief in the ghosts
Who lived with him in his home.
The quartz in the stone
It was built with wouldn't
Let them out, he explained,
Fearless in ways few of us are.
I wish he would have called.
We could have smoked cigars together
And once again solved nothing,
The same way we always used to.
So I drove past his old house
Just a little while ago and
Of course saw no ghosts.
But I noticed one thing
Odd in the middle of the afternoon,
On that first day he wouldn't return:
Everything seemed quiet
And the porch light was on

Unforgettable Things I Always Forget

In the sepia dawn of an ordinary February day
The clouds form a kind of Braille alphabet,
Soon worn down by the sun coming over the hill
That has graciously and without much drama
Always held everything intact here

Exhaling whatever dream I had, I remain still in bed,
Watching the end of these tricks of shadows
Pantomime a paradigm of winter's peculiar mood,
Crossing ceiling and wall in slow motion,
Impenetrable as a clever enemy code

The noise of traffic already starting to erode the morning
Out on the highway, not a mile off through the windows
I wake to, and through the mutating shades
Of beige and gray, I note with quiet glee
Those renegade streaks of mauve and indigo

I hear the sound of a stream without water,
The rush of air through a busted tube,
While trying to read a diagram without a plan,
Perhaps like instructions a psycho would include
In a toy set no one would want to play with

And yet I have to rise and dress to re-memorize
The unforgettable things I always forget,
One of which is that movement alone is an end to seek,
Even if it's toward gathering more of what we cannot hold,
And away from just noticing what we could never invent

In Lieu of an Autobiography

I could write enough to fill a hefty volume, for sure,
Even without excessive adjectives, running on,
Like those adolescent essays due tomorrow.
But truly, a lot of the action would be slow

Nonetheless, it'd be an interesting tale, at least,
Even omitting most of the flattering revisions
And many of the more embarrassing positions.
Every guy loves to tell the story of himself

Yes, the dirty details would be thrilling to some,
Maybe even make it sell, perhaps as a screenplay
For one of those "Based on True Events" movies,
But I'd rather not go into them

It's my autobiography, after all, and I'll say what I want.
I suppose I could call it "Historical Fiction," but then
I'd have to change the names or else worry
About lawsuits and other recriminations

It wouldn't make any money anyway. It wouldn't be
One of those blockbusters or best sellers, so why bother?
That always seemed to be the point to everything
For almost everyone I ever talked to along the way

Although it never was for me.
The kinds of things I like to do don't really pay.
And with that being the case, the plot would contain
Dull references to drowning in debt, being profligate

The pyrrhic ways of a ne'er-do-well
Who believed a pile of pages stacked high enough
Might reach his sorry ass to heaven.
And that's the main part I'm still uncertain about

The heaven element: I haven't yet come to terms
With those sorts of notions—you know, the next place
And all that, the spiritualism. But therein hides the theme,
In the redundancy of the action-less scenes

The bland saga of a guy from Scranton, looking for meaning
In the streets and alleys of a place filled with religion,
His madcap adventures and mischievous encounters
As he aged beyond anyone's expectations

In the melancholy end, though, he fails in his unnamed quest,
And the heroic portrayal of an incorrigible brat just fades out.
Everyone is let down again, sensing there is no redemption.
Too many questions would linger, the sort with no answers.
Even if I decided to fill in the gaping blanks with prurient truths,
We all know there's a very limited audience for epics like that

Bells from Different Towers

The bells don't ring together
Off their unison by a heartbeat
At noon

Twenty-four knells tells us precisely
How easily
Things can go wrong

Heirlooms

Grail

If there is some veiled answer
It may as well be in Scranton

Not so glamorous
But neither was the grail

A list of preferable cities
Would likely be quite long to most people

They'd be cleaner and nicer
And have more excitement going on

It's not a popular town,
The brunt of many cinematic jokes

But I'm not so popular either
So it suits me where I'm bred

Maybe it's in my blood
Or just some self-taught belief

I think it was William Carlos Williams who said
Everything you need is in your own backyard

And he was from New Jersey so he knew
What he meant to look around wherever you are

The buildings here aren't fancy and a lot of the landscape
Is scarred from the greed of a history of whores

Protected by churches and mayors still festooning
The area like open sores on an otherwise fine body

But the nights are beautiful, the glitter of the lights
Down the valley, and everything you ever have to see

In the brave, disgruntled faces that wait for buses amid litter
Blowing to the corners of the magical streets downtown

It Was All Green Once

Where you see the ground turned
Across the hilltops there
Right where those rusty wire towers rise
From the gray rocks laid bare
In the cause of the power plant
Far south along the river
Dried now to a trickling stream
To heat and light places far away from here
It was all green once

And with the seasons
The trees would change colors
Extravagantly
Before the hollow metal winter
Rolled in on huge yellow machines
Over what was all green once

They used helicopters to string the lines
After they ran a wide swath of fire to kill
Permanently
The oaks and maples and locusts and ash
That blended together in lovely months
And made it all green once

And there on the other side of the valley
The landfill has grown the size of a city
With the constant traffic of trucks full of trash
From New Jersey weighing in at the cash gates
Securely enclosing a forbidden place
That was all green once

The history of coal mines beneath us
Left us standing here on a thin crust
Like too many toys on a bowing shelf
Complete with quaint trains that circle
And every once in a while a sinkhole
Might open up to swallow a dusty house
Amid a little garden that was all green once

But aside from the culm piles and slag hills
Which have grown their own scrub birch beards
To mostly cover their dirty faces
Over the past century or so
And masquerade as something else entirely
Between all these beaten towns
Still littered with stray dreams of beauty
At least it was all green once

Bargain

It may not be an emergency,
But in November, from this hill to that other,
There is clearly a sense of sepia urgency

Choking on the endless traffic out on the highway,
This little valley in between,
Whose emerald mouth of summer
Has now become a brittle, brown maw,
Unable to swallow anything more

Catastrophe exists in everything, waiting,
This deviant inertia, a latent plague,
Incalculable with our domesticated mathematics,
Incurable through our cataracts toward ruin

This path to disaster was tamed long ago
By the desperate ancestors of this place,
Who spooned out their own rib cage for warm ash

This time of year, you can also see
The massive junkyard and the threadbare rise
Of the busy landfill from here

Both owned by the dour billionaire
Who lives right over there,
Not a mile away as the crow flies

He drives past my house early each day,
Ignoring the stop signs up the street,
Twice, on his way to and from morning Mass
At the big church downtown

Where forgiveness for anything is dispensed
In doubtless confessionals at the bargain expense
Of some rote words and regular tithes

Winks and Nods

Staked and tied with wires
Draped along one side
Of the valley's hilltops
Undermined
To strip out the coal
A hundred years ago

So now we can build
A mountain of garbage
To complete the bleak
Enclosure of our world

Exposed again by our need
To accept pittances at the expense
Of what we hold dear

We will sell it all
To the barons whose greed
Apparently knows no end
To whom history has always provided
A private back door

Like the dime whores
Who lured the dried-out sailors here
From the home front shores
In a heyday we took
All the wrong lessons from

While the duly elected sit silent
As they've always done around here
Waiting for their winks and nods to pay

South Side Christmas Village

Down past the ammunition plant
With its high walls and gates,
Following the overhead wires that run
The full length of the pitted road
In front of the Salvation Army rehab center,
Through power transformers that hang like torsos
From militant poles

Past the crude bell-ringing Santa Claus
Calling out for change,
Beside the South Side Shopping Plaza
Near the bowling lanes, and straight out
To the remains of the Capitol Records building,
Where The Beatles and The Beach Boys pressed
Their names into vinyl history,
Next to the crumbling brick remnants
Of one of Scranton's famous old silk mills,
Both long since boarded and closed

Over the rusted railroad tracks they built
This country with, which once brought in coal cars
To fill with the groans of struggling miners,
And then hauled the bones of their wealth away

On either side of the street by the tobacco stores,
Lottery tickets litter the sidewalks
In yet another series of losses, scratched off
And discarded, with the brief dreams they bought
Of new carpeting or a fishing boat perhaps

The people look like hapless dead, walking along
In December, with their hooded faces down,
Under holiday decorations left up through the soot
Of at least one year gone, in a calendar without pages,
The frayed wreaths and dusty red and green
Season's Greetings garland buntings,
Dangling by thin nooses of twine

No one looks up
At the slate gray sky in the dusk
That bends down to lid this late afternoon hour,
Surrounding the whole scene like a smoked-glass dome

Like a savagely shaken gift shop globe,
Now still on a dusty, cluttered shelf,
With no snowflakes floating in its liquid air
To finish off the simile one might hope to find here
Of a miniature Christmas village

An enchanting little place
That could somehow be said to seem
Peaceful or useful or sacred or quaint

December Decorations

Rows of pointed rooftops like pews of hands in prayer
Line the street. Smoke billows like incense from their chimneys.
Another December, consecrated in sepia tones,
Like an old newspaper photograph.
Stigmata of a dried out past in streaks of soot
Beneath the gables like tracks of silt tears
Or spilt blood

All of these houses, built at a time when the fabled silk mills
And coal mines worked furiously
To clothe and heat those in places far away

Railroad tracks run empty across the creek by the baseball fields
Out back, where history was made by generations of boys
Who played around those diamonds
For trophies permanently displayed in an infinity of mirrors
Behind the brown bottles of neighborhood bars

Where the cars in the lots are old models with backseats
Worn threadbare from memories the gray whiskered men inside
Still hold close and swap over shots and beers

Recalling the stories of kids who made good
And their sisters who married well and moved
To cities where the sidewalks are swept and clean

How they come home to visit around these holidays
With children who ask nothing of how it was
In the old days anymore

Whose eyes glass over if they hear one more thing
About hospital stays or local political races

Even the yellowing tales of running those same bases
As golden young heroes The Scranton Times once covered
Hold no grandeur for grandchildren who have had the world
Handed to them like an unearned reward

As dusk falls, the strands of lights, annually strung
From peeling banisters around porches people used to sit on
When the weather permitted, circling the cold figures
Of nativity scenes brought down from the attic,
Flicker to life in dull colored bulbs

Which still mean something to the ones who remain,
Who drape these decorations in frantically shortened days,
In the pageless bloodline calendar of this great place,
Whether anyone notices them now or not

Christmas Thought of Karl Marx

The girl puts the goods in the bag
Which I carry away by delicate handles,
Neither of us considering the makers
Of either the goods in the bag
Or the bag itself. Self-consciously,
I walk through the mall, hurriedly
Back to my car, not thinking of Karl Marx
Right now, or any fetish aside from escape
Into the fading commodity of crowdlessness,
Blessed with the holy scrolls of rolled receipts
And a selfish relief for a chore now done.
Yet somewhere, I suddenly surmise,
In circumstances I would deplore and despise,
Someone grossly underpaid with aching fingers
Is making more of whatever it is in my bag,
While someone else, somewhere else,
Labors to make another bag

On the Funeral of a Stranger

Behind a tall fence made of spears
And black gates that swing inward,
A procession of cars oozed through
The brown cemetery to a dirt mound

The dull shine of the gray hearse
Led a slow parade of purple flags
On cars to a canopied grave beside
A headstone of granite names

From my distance, the monotone
Of prayers sounded like a dark wind.
The bowed heads nodded in unison
Over something that was being said

I recalled the many times I stood
In similar places in scenes like this,
Over the various dead of my own history,
And how I felt with my head down then

Grateful now to be just a random witness
Who happened to stop briefly to watch this,
I caught a glimpse of the lineage of man
In the grim circle of those standing around

The frailty and strength of our rites,
The way nice words spoken in a drone
Hope to ease us from pains for which
There is only a temporary escape

Even when we can't hear them clearly,
And they're not meant particularly for us,
They reach through the endless sky,
Filling that breach between what is real
For those other people at this moment
And what has been and will be for us again

Requiem for My First Friend

I'm sure I have a memory of meeting you the first time,
In our strollers with our mothers on the sidewalk
We would soon grow to own

There are those pictures in a shoebox
Of games we played in the yard, my helmet on backwards
In one; you swinging higher in another

You tied my shoes for me until the third grade
And never even spread it around as a taunt
For other kids in our class to laugh

The time we slit our fingers with a pocketknife
To mingle blood and become brothers
The way we knew Indians did

And today, so many years away from it
I went through a Mass for you in the same pews
We held our breath, fearing the loud monsignor

He wasn't there either. And I wonder
How far you were from the savior they keep slaying.
The priest confessed he didn't even know you

Then, emerging from the church into sunlight
Like the day of our First Communion, another picture
In the shoebox, I blinked off my loss of angels

And drove in the parade to your grave.
Though you disappeared in mystery and so much
About you is unknown to me now, all this time later

I have to believe that any good god would save
A decent place somewhere in all the infinity he rules
For the likes of you

Wonder about a Wanderer

There's a guy who walks around
Downtown these days, talking to himself,
Often stopping and turning to shout
At whoever he believes is behind him

Dressed as a gray refugee, the possibly once-neat
Hair and beard, long gone feral, ever since
Whatever fateful event triggered his current state.
I followed him for a few blocks just the other day

To see if I could find out what he meant,
But I couldn't, so I had to surmise. It might have been
And unfinished argument, maybe one he walked away from,
And then just kept walking, taking her last resonating phrase

Along with him to drag like a dogging tail. At times, he flails
His arms in the air, scattering the bad words he hears,
Cursing loudly, suddenly startling so many passersby.
I imagine him rising from a table, swallowing a final

Mouthful of anxiety before storming out, leaving the door
Of the house wide open in his wake. Locked now
In a ceaseless conversation, the hard dialogue echoing,
Repeating in his head like a terrible jingle, haunting

His relentless sidewalk march, to no single destination,
No ultimate point of return, no quarters of comfort
Or care or concern, although neither I, nor anyone else,
Attempt to approach him to learn the details

Under the Sidewalk

I saw him there, crouching,
I guess just before he died,
As I headed through his alley,
A shortcut to somewhere else

Not a hundred feet from city hall,
From a recess beneath a raised sidewalk
Where a building had once been,
Now another vacant lot, he peered out

He saw me see him, watched me
With eyes squinting like a miner's,
Unaccustomed to sun, awkward
Even in this old coal town

At the time I thought I should write it down,
And later that night I talked with friends
About the curious man and his sad domain,
Surmising a glib myth of his hours

In the paper the next day, coincidentally,
There was a picture of a makeshift cross
Someone cared enough to stick in the dirt
Beside his toppled shopping cart

Things Repurposed

The old silk mill
Built of brick long ago
In the dell beside Roaring Brook
Just across the railroad tracks from here

To make stockings and scarves
For the rich and parachutes for the army
Has been converted to loft apartments
Always with vacancy signs

No one around here
Wears soft garments anymore anyway
It's all nylon and cotton and denim
Made in places far away

Brought in on trucks
By the highway constructed
Just above the factory structure
Where women took over the work

Once the men had shipped off
To the war
Leaving everything behind
And returning to find everything

Changed
Even their stories
Sorrowfully told now
At the empty end of days

The narrative glory mutated
To shadowy conversations
In the gray domain
Of those neighborhood bars
Which remain
The only things that still do
The very thing they were made to

Pockets of Immigrants

There was the old sod
The emerald island
They came in boats from
No one in my family remembers when
The specific year doesn't matter
Anyway
They got here and followed mules
Down into the black ground
Deep past anything green
To hollow out a new salvation
To trade under the posted rules
Of the company store
Owned by the bosses they worked for
Or put on blue uniforms
To march with sharp bayonets south
Against rebels they had no grudge against
And ride with canvas sacks of regret
On rumbling trains back
If they survived that war
To resume their place in the line
That was the life of expendable men
Each of whom had an infant die
Each one a wife in a housedress
With messy hair and a cameo locket
All of them had pants pockets
They couldn't put their hands in
Because there was never time
To just stand around like that
And nothing to pull out of there
Anyway

The Silver Chalice

The silver chalice
As far back as I can remember
Stood on top of the curio cabinet
My parents had in the living room

Ornate and engraved
With the initials of my great grandfather
A gift from the king
Is how the story goes

Brought here no one knows when
From the ebbing glory of the Swedish kingdom

Advised never to try to clean it
For fear of tainting a different kind of value
Than what it truly provides
It stands now on a shelf in our house in Scranton

Tarnished like everything else
However grand
From history
As a child I imagined

An epochal ceremony
An ermine-cloaked monarch with a golden crown
Bequeathing it upon my ancestor
Who modestly bowed to accept it

A thousand years from the Viking age
Still I envisioned a hero
Who sailed to America in a dragon boat
Wrapped in fur and armed with a sword

But really he was just a scientist
Who invented a powder to blow things up
And left behind this storied cup to adorn
The lineage of homes we've occupied ever since

Reminding us whenever we bother to look at it
That any imagined lore is inevitably contrived
To be heroic and glamorous
And may even incent us

Toward a mythic existence
More useful in this universe
Than whatever the actual reality was
Of our forefathers' forgotten lives

The Missing Sword

Where does one's history actually begin?
It's so hard to know such things about yourself.
The branches of your lineage, all the way back,
Through the lost traces of the first sperm and egg,
A million times removed from whatever primordial goo
Made you into whatever you are today

I can say it didn't start in 1698,
The furthest date I could find in my cheap research,
And there's no way to be sure of any of that,
Or of what may have happened before then.
In my case, a Swedish man met an Irish lass,
And a Welsh lad met a Frau, and these four combined
To make my mom and dad somehow

It's all conjecture, left to me and my sisters to decide what to say.
But we've surmised we can blame our love of liquor, and the way
Our eyes can quickly turn cold and hard, on our bloodline,
And those deeper angers that rise like slow tides in us
Have an unmistakably Germanic flair to them,
Matched with our Viking intolerance for the civilized balance
Of the way things are, then mixed with a melancholic Celtic twist,
To lilt the music we choose to explain ourselves with

No one could ever state with certainty where our name came from.
We were told it has to do with flowers, most recognizable along
The Baltic Coasts. And that sort of makes sense, since in my heart
I love flowers—how they look and what they mean.
I'll gladly hold out a nice bouquet as a sign of friendship and peace,
Usually to those I must appease.
But always with my left hand

You see, my right, I like to keep that one free, however subconsciously.
I believe that it's a deep intuition, an instinct, one might say, inbred,
Just in case I'm ever compelled to reach for the missing sword,
The one that should still hang from my belt, ready when needed,
Even today, through all the blending and dilution, the sanctification
And civilization of my earliest, more heathen roots

Sepia Still Life

In their dusty frames, generations away,
Long dead and all but forgotten,
Except for the pictures in these boxes,
Moved around so many times.
My Swedish ancestors, in baroque rooms
Of Stockholm, dressed like fabled Jarls and wives,
I watch them hypnotically.
Someday I must decide to hang them,
Once I know I'll be around in the same house,
At least for a little while.
I surmise that they'd like Scranton,
This sepia town where buttoned vests
Draw much attention,
And each man is his own peninsula,
Whose grandparents told stories
Of the Old World, before America,
Where grandeur was measured differently,
And there was a continuity you could breathe.
They've lived in our attics for too long now,
From one house to the next, through moves
And divorces and deaths. They need me to free them
By securing them to a wall at last,
As they have secured me to a vague history,
A past, none of us really knows about, words of mouth
Having been muted by the crashing waves of time.
I note curiously the similarities of features we share,
And sometimes I believe I can read their minds,
Hear them speak in a language intuitively known
Through their soundless echoes.
They don't always have the kindest thoughts either,
Nor are they the sort to appreciate change,
Which may be why I've just left them in their box
Through all the things gone wrong,
Visiting them only sporadically, accidentally
For the most part, coming across them
At such odd moments in my life.
I don't even know all of their names,
But I like that they posed for these brown photographs

To remind me these many years later
That I've never been alone in my face,
And that the wistful scowl people say I often wear
Has a fine lineage, going all the way back
To a far more glorious kingdom than this

Genealogy

Where will it lead back to?

You shouldn't even ask
Because somewhere in the past
In some branch of the tree
Of the line you come from
You'll always find at least one
Disastrous ancestor

And if you can't
Then you should know in advance
That somewhere down the road
Others searching for their roots
Will surely find one

And it will have to be you

Road Rage in the Backyard

I am in a mood
To bemoan the lack
Of courtesy in our world.
In Europe they are still
Killing people for race and
Religion and things like that.
Young mothers in Utah
Stuff dead babies into hampers
Like laundry they don't want to do.
In the mountains out there
There are camps training children
To wipe out the survivors
Of some war they desire to start.
The army and navy store
Can't keep up with the demand
For combat boots and camouflage,
The barrage of requests for more
Ammunition and bigger guns.
How do people ever with straight faces
Say they soldier for God,
Whose own legion is grass and trees?
Nazis are romanticized
In prison cells in Texas
Where the death bed
Is in the shape of a cross.
The loss of civility is a casualty
We cannot bear to the next hilltop
Of our slag pile history.
My own feelings swing
Like a lynching victim now
As I suddenly wish to go over there
With the nearest weapon at hand
And crush my rude neighbor's
Constantly barking dogs

Trophy of Old Age

The mirror
A display case
For your trophy

Your face
Changed with each
Yellow reward

Not for heroics necessarily
Nor for conquests or victories
But merely for making it here

Where you gaze
At the lines your seasons
Recorded in deep creases

Your eyes and teeth
The skin of your cheeks
The uncertainty of your lips

All hold those weary stories
Your tongue longs to tell someone
Of the good things you have done

But even you don't want to listen
To yourself anymore
Your empty and unconvincing words

At last you might look away
Once you formalize a truce
And are able to make yourself believe

Your phases have been the finest awards
You've won and how your losses
Ultimately become you

You can release yourself
From your broken smile now
And settle for an awkward peace

Because it seems you've at least
Attained an age you never dreamed of
And worn yourself out fairly well

The Funeral of Aunt Fran

The arches of stained glass
Torch magnificent streaks of orange
Across the ceaseless Jesus
And the small crowd gathered here
In this baroque cathedral
For the funeral of Aunt Fran

The vast organ in the loft
Wails through huge golden pipes
The closing of her beauty salon
After fifty years doing hair

The chanting priest swings
A smoking canister until the air
Is ruined and they roll her coffin out

Doubtless in her ancient vows
To the ubiquitous church
This one hidden on a corner in South Side
And to my crazy uncle she wed long ago
Whose own father hated the pope
And all the rest of the Church of Rome

Yet even he would have to marvel at this
The slashes of light across glass shards of saints
All in a row and the bone drilling pain
Of that instrument's sustained notes
Whose voice it seems is neither choked
By the gray billows of incense
Nor relieved by the ceremonial glory
Of this most ordinary death

Heirloom

Methodically she had placed
The adhesive tabs that came with it
On the appropriate pages
Of the gilded heirloom bible
She sent away for

Color-coded and neatly in line
Like a well disciplined army
Marking the passages
Those television evangelists
Said mattered most

She kept certain photos
And fifty dollar bills
Inside the cover of this special book
Which remained until the end
On the table beside her bed
Where she waited for my father
Who forever said he had his own
Arrangement with the Lord

I'm pretty sure he never read it
And to my knowledge
Because the TV was always on
Neither did she

Apologies

Castle

Just the other day I was
A kid with a castle to build

Without instructions
I made mistakes constructing it

But by the time anyone noticed
The drawbridge was already up

And I was safe inside
With my loyal army of childish hopes

Guarding the walls
This side of the dividing moat

Where I still wait for myself at times
To join me again today

I Wasn't There When They Made the Rules

All through school they told me—
Usually but not always as a quiet aside—
There's something wrong with you.
That Catholic psychologist
Made me flip when I was a kid.
Son of a bitch, I thought,
You get hit by those nuns regularly
And see how your moods swing.
All I ever did was burn down
The garage and throw some things
Across the room.
You know, they checked my pockets
For matches and stolen goods
Until I moved away.
And yes, I will now confess,
I ate that basket of holy wafers
From the church on a dare.
By the way, if you care to know,
They taste like shit.
Also—and no one else knows this—I did
Lust after the neighbor's daughter and wife
Simultaneously.
Was that crazy?
I guess, if you say so,
But at least I admit it.
And yet, here I am now, sort of all right,
If a bit hazy at times about it all.
And as to those thoughts
Which have never really stopped,
I can only argue that
Since I wasn't there when they made the rules,
It's not really fair to point at me

Poetry and Math

In school they taught poetry
Like math

You could count out the breaths
And crack the code they told you about
For the algebraic tests with questions
That left everything about it for dead

I got kicked out
Of both classes

They said I couldn't add very well
And wouldn't sit still long enough
To grasp the concepts they fed

In the empty hall the long corridor
At each end a beckoning door
You had to choose or else report
To the office for more raised brows
And detentions and suspensions
And explanations blah blah blah

So instead I'd skip outside
Where the sky has no equation
And you can divide the clouds
Any way you see fit and the birds
Who live there don't even mind

And I'd escape both sides for a while
At least until the next day when my name
Would boom over the PA system
Like a loud wanted poster

And the echoes of that became
The sound of the sum of line breaks
Multiplying and dividing
The years ever since
Into one long uncorrectable poem

Reason to Pay Attention in Auto Shop

The mechanics of engines has always been beyond me.
Pistons, transmissions, cams, the arcane tangles of hoses
And wires; I confess, I just don't understand it all,
Which is a difficult admission for a man
Who's had so many cars through the years

I should've paid slight attention in auto shop,
But the guys who took that class with me seemed intuitively
Aligned just by listening, geared like automotive savants,
Lingering as they would at any open hood, unafraid
To stick their fingers in and poke around with silver tools

They used to scoff at fools like me, dilettantes
To whom even windshield wipers, with their timers and sensors,
Were a challenge, satisfied with my belief that the ignition key,
Through some magical coalescence of combustion
And secrets of greasy engineering, simply brought the motor to life

And it never mattered much to me back then, or now really,
As long as the thing started and ran, and the stereo gave sound.
Until one day, some parenthetical aspect of the equation fails
And there's just a tick-tick-ticking when there should be a roar,
And even before I finish giving my opinion to the tow truck guy

He smugly smiles and gives me a wink, saying something
About the fly wheel, which he seems to think is funny.
"Is that a big deal?" I ask, naïve as a lost foreigner
With the wrong city map. "Not if you have the money,"
He replies, wiping his hands on a rag

My spirit sags as in a puff of smoke he hauls my ride away
To that grimy laboratory, where those same boys
I once skip-roped jumper cables with in the high school garage
Will close the big door and wave their wands to fix my car,
And later present to me an itemized bill I can't even read

Guilt Comes Later

I felt a pang of guilt
As I read the obituary
Of the former high school teacher
I tormented all those years ago,
His picture instantly recognizable
Among the other faces of death,
Those daily fixtures in the morning paper.
Apparently he had a life
I cared nothing about,
Heedless in myopic teenage ways,
Back in those days when it was a mistake
To try to tell me about something like geometry,
A kid who believed in the righteousness of doodling,
Giving meaning to angles a whole different way.
Maybe he was some kind of hero in a war
Before he ever met a brat like me.
Maybe there were people who loved him.
Surely he had troubles as we all grow to own.
Over coffee now I can only surmise,
Reminded how we all die sometime,
And how those who were brutal to us
May drag certain regrets through their lives,
And how perhaps it is only a lack of notice
We forever rue the most

Translating Catullus

I wouldn't even remember how
To begin translating Catullus now
Without the worn Latin dictionary
Balanced like an egg upon my knee

In college I stayed up really late,
Drank a lot of coffee and ate
Anything romantic. A broken heart
Was always the best place to start

It's true, I got terrible grades,
Always more interested in the parades
Of girls swishing in between classes,
Which I couldn't even see today without glasses

Yet something nested in me, like that sparrow
He fretted about, deep in my marrow,
And ever since it has been a feathered agony,
Always finding new ways to pick at me

I remember reciting what I thought he said,
To which the professor would slowly shake his head,
And I'd walk back through the millennia to my dorm
Chased by that ancient poet's dark winged form

For the Professor Who Neglected Hart Crane

The Modern Poetry course I took in college
Skipped right over poor Hart Crane,
Focusing instead with margin notes
And test questions on many other poets,
Few so wracked with pain, and fewer still
So decisively dead

Years later, in the warm torn elbow covert
Of a bookshop I found a paperback
Of his collected works like a smoking souvenir—
A thin volume (of course, he died quite young),
And I've wondered ever since why,
By that professor, he was left untouched

One who spends himself out again,
Each line a caustic drop strung in harmony,
A perfect cry, like rain on an attic rooftop,
Cruel as the bottom of the sea, through which we,
In our bedlamite sanctioning of the sun,
May once gaze toward paradise and notice

If only for a moment, a myth of God, and see
The fabulous shadow of that inevitable thumb,
Made by the moon in lonely alleys, and hear
From an empty ash can we might witness there
A grail of laughter spread like scalding unguents
Through gaiety and quest, a kitten in the wilderness

Kafkaesque

I played a Franz Kafka character today,
Well dressed in a fitting suit,
Being directed from one room
To another, full of serious people

I sat in the back, making notes
That had nothing to do with the teachings.
I covered them with my hand so no one would see
What was really going on in my head

When I was called upon to answer,
I unwillingly envisioned a dung beetle instead,
And paused just long enough for them all
To throw apples at me

Not apples, really, but scowls and sneers,
And coffee cups and pens,
And when it was over, I sat with my wounds,
Not even hearing myself protest

As they led me away by the arms,
I remembered what I should have said,
But by then I guess it was too late to recover,
And they placed me in a faithless grave

Out in the parking lot,
Alongside a few others
Who apparently didn't know
What the wrong thing was either

Sorry

To everyone I owe an apology to
Although you may not know who you are

The recipient of some slight of mine
Or outright victim of a past crime

Going through your lives
Without proper closure

You may not even have been aware
We both need to be set free

Of the weight of my misdeeds
At the risk of opening old wounds

Maybe it was your daughter or your wife
Or girlfriend or property

It's hard to decide now
So many years later

I don't even remember too clearly
How some of those things happened

In the back rooms and alleys of my youth
When I didn't look past that night's moon

But I have an urge to express my regrets
Whether I felt them then or not

Sitting here today in the peace
Of one who has gotten away with it

Don't ask for a purge of details
I don't seek your forgiveness

I'll just say this that the older I get
The sorrier I feel for some of the stuff I did

Pain in the Neck

The spot right at the top of my spine
Is sore all the time these days
Like a spike is stuck in it

Maybe it's from driving a lot
Or sitting hunched at a desk or stress
Or not getting massages often enough

I'm not a hypochondriac and I don't think
I've done that much wrong in my life.
It's not like I'm really old or anything;
Actually I'm in pretty good physical shape

But I saw a movie once where someone
Was bent down under a weigh and none
Of the doctors could determine what it was

It turned out somehow to be a cargo
Of bad ghosts riding on the person's back,
Digging their nails into their victim's neck

Although I don't remember the story too clearly
Or how they discovered the cause of the malady,
There was no cure for the poor bastard

And something about the end of the film,
The grim moral of the story, how the evils
You've done add up to equal a terminal burden
You carry for the rest of your days,
Made me believe they were leaving room
For one of those unendurable sequels
No one ever goes to see

My Friend Gives Up Hunting

His fine rifles recline in a nice glass case
Having done their dirty duty over the years;
The deer heads on his rec room walls
Strange trophies of an urge he recently retired

"I just don't want to kill anything
Anymore," he said. "I don't know why
I've changed." Now even groundhogs are safe
To leave their holes out in his yard

I sit with him at his bar,
The taxidermied buck watching our every move.
We've been friends for a very long time
And I've never seen him mad

He can't explain his revelation further,
This epiphany that keeps him out of the woods
These days, perhaps informed somehow
By the silent horned heads around us

Whose eyes follow like an optical trick,
Their ears propped up with sawdust to listen.
He didn't feel too good about the last one
He shot, even though he always had
The good meat professionally cut
And delivered to the hungry poor

Vignette of My Father

Smoke swirled in gray elegance
Around his face, his quick hands
Flicking at an ashtray,
Lifting up a glass to pray

Handsome and always well dressed,
Perfectly knotted and vested,
Comfortable at any bar,
A winner at witty repartee

His smile wouldn't fade until after
He was in the car alone, his laughter
Then turned into a long coughing spasm,
Driving back over the wide chasm

From the kingdom of strangers
To the familiar place where changes
Are harder to direct and control
And just being there can take a hefty toll

In that place we called home
Where we all lived together alone

Loyalty Oath

How was I to know
Whether he was drunk or not?
It all seemed ordinary to me,
Riding in the back seat
On the way home, as I always did.
I didn't notice any swerving
Or anything that wasn't routine,
So all I could do was shrug
When the lawyer asked
Whose fault I thought it was.
I was only about seven anyway,
A kid—not serving as a good
Eye witness for either side.
But even if I knew for certain
My dad was in the wrong,
I would have lied,
With no need for coaxing,
Because I learned early on
Some of the oaths I still believe in
Are different from the flawed kinds
You recite out loud.
You don't hold your hand
On a book for them, or swear to God,
And they have nothing whatsoever
To do with judges or courts or laws

A History of Flowers

My mother never liked to receive flowers,
Neither roses nor assorted bouquets,
Not for holidays, birthdays, or anniversaries.
She was odd that way

She always said she didn't like to see them
Wither, when they slumped over
With that sad brown trim.
Of course, artificial flowers were beneath her,
So the only ones ever in the house were those
In the painting made by my great aunt the nun
Who had joined the convent as a very young girl
(Married to Jesus, I remember being surprised
To learn), and turned old in a convent
In the petals of a long black robe

My father, I'm sure, would have given them routinely,
Even outside of any scheme for forgiveness,
Which he often needed; but in deference to my mother,
He never did

I brought some to his death bed,
Strategically placed them right at eye level for him.
Between struggling breaths near the end,
He said they were beautiful.
And after he finally went,
Mom quietly confessed she kind of liked them, too

My Sister's Collages

When she started to make collages,
Even better codes than poetry,
No one would know those images,
Glued from random pages
To canvas and given arcane names
Framed her silent explosions

No sense in listing in words
Torments best left unspoken,
Relentless now on the walls
Where I've hung them
Which close in without explanation
Whenever I think about it

A veritable history in paper shards,
Impenetrable as the runes we come from,
That say what need to be said
Without ever being truly understood,
The same way lost civilizations
Still taunt us with their dark clues

The Real Estate

A lovely home in a nice neighborhood
      The hall is long and dark
      Whenever I'm wrong
A heated garage with electric doors
      The stairs are steep
      Whenever I'm late
A beautifully landscaped and well tended yard
      The trees even tremble
      Whenever I've failed
A white picket fence with a quaint latching gate
      The squirrels run away
      From what I forgot
A red cedar mailbox at the end of the walk
      The sky is still blue
      When I lose another job
A fine brass lamp illuminates the stoop
      A smile like starlight
      From a far distant past
A large bay window to master the view
      The shoes by the door
      Have shit on their soles
A young couple waves as they pass down the street
      The fine brick façade
      Of a desirable world

White Rugs and Metaphors

Never buy a white carpet for your house,
Regardless of how your subconscious might beg
For something pure. It won't stay that way
For very long, unless you decide to never go anywhere

It might be a difficult conversation to have
With your wife, who may insist on wanting a white rug
To cover the floor, but don't be drawn in to explain
Any metaphors; just stand firm on its impracticality

Even the simile of beige is up for debate, but at least with that
You're already halfway to the certain ruin of it all,
And you can be sure that somewhere down the road
She'll tacitly agree that you were right

Of course, she may never say so, or admit
That your decorating skills are superior to hers.
Don't expect anything more than a nod of agreement
When your turn to vacuum the fucking thing comes around

Final Apology

After the many routine disputations
That ranged from every bad thing
I ever did to every bad thing
I'll ever do
The words finally just ran out
And a pulsing silence
Took their place

Although each tirade itself
About my broken parts
Never ended
The redundant phrases
Started to be spoken
Only in facial expressions

The questions were always
Rhetorical
Categorical condemnations
Of behaviors that must be
Encoded in my DNA

I just repeated
"Sorry" again and again
Like amen
At the end of a long prayer

I did contribute
"But But But"
Here and there

Which is where we left it
Changing venues
After all the papers were signed

And all these years later
In the measure of quiet
I've been able to find
Away from the immolating rants
I've decided to forgive myself
Offering this one final apology
To the indifferent air
That may carry it forth forever
Through the heedless sky from here
Because I've come to understand
At last
I'm really not that bad of a guy

A Crowded Shelf

for My Sister, Karen

On that shelf over there
All these books with her name on them
And a thousand others she read
Left here better than any monument

In the air around them
The kinds of things she said
Quiet as a page turning in candlelight
I can still discern each of her tones

The mountain of papers unread
Burned at her stern request
Just before she fled this jurisdiction
Left us to guess her other confessions

I've imagined every story I can
Every permutation of those ashes
Of maybe this or maybe that
Happening in my sister's private life

And now when I ask she is silent
Which is easier for the dead
Wanting me only to make her ghost laugh again
Which of course I still try to do

And to be quiet long enough to finally understand
There are many things
Even those we feel a yearning need to say
No one else ever really needs to know

Everyone Loves a Funny Guy

We all crack up,
It's only a matter of when
A particular thing or
Sequence of events triggers
A breach and the relentlessly
Stable mind rocks off kilter,
And you find yourself filling in
The blanks of the crazy uncle
You knew you had
But no one ever discussed.
We all go mad,
It's just a matter of how mad,
How glibly we can flip from joy
To sadness and back again
In an instant,
The distance between rants
And whether you catch yourself
Chanting odd phrases in public.
Sooner or later someone will ask
Why,
So have a deadpan reply ready,
Something that will make them
Laugh,
Because people like that
And they'll usually give you a pass
If they think you're funny

The Old Man in the Mirror

I was talking to a gruff old man,
Smoking a cigar right in my face

There are lots of such guys around here,
Most in every mirror, I'd say

He was telling me as I was talking
How everything seems to go wrong eventually

Not like in the old days that never were
When everything was better than it is now

When everything was the way it should be
Back in those old days that never were

We both sighed and shrugged together,
Our shoulders sore like twin brothers

"It's all just one more thing," he said,
Moving my lips like a reluctant puppet

"How did you get your hand up my ass
To control me, old man?" I asked angrily

I could see by his smirk and the gleam
In his eye, he was devising a clever reply

I tasted the long puff he took, briefly lost
In the smoke of his answer on my behalf

He spoke not only for me, but for all old men
Who finally get around to that bereft question

It made me feel kind of sorry for him, though,
Like maybe wise crack jokes were all he had left

"You bent over once too many times," he laughed.
"And now you know there's no going back," he said

About the Author

Tom Blomain was born in Scranton in 1957, attending parochial school until his family moved to the suburb of Clarks Summit, where he went to public school. There, he was part of a crew named Most Mischievous in their high school yearbook. His record for suspensions may still stand today. He attended nearby Keystone Junior College and graduated from Dickinson College. He was founding editor of the short-lived *Northeast Magazine,* before following in his family-line business of insurance, acquiring various professional designations in the industry, while remaining active in the region's arts community. His first book of poems entitled *Gray Area* was published by Nightshade Press in 2004, for which he also served as editor of the subsequent *5 Poets* collection. His second book, *Blues From Paradise,* was released by Foothills Publishing in 2014. His poetry has also appeared in several anthologies and periodicals. A songwriter, reasonably good singer and guitar player, he also writes stories and likes to draw. Occasionally, he co-produces a poetry and music show called *Graffiti* for Electric City Television. He lives in Scranton's historic Hill Section with his wife, Jessica.

9 781630 450298